I Was Just A To Go To Bed

D1063186

written by
Lucy McClymont

illustrated by
Wallace Keller

HARCOURT BRACE & COMPANY

Orlando Atlanta Austin Boston San Francisco Chicago Dallas New York
Toronto London

I was just about to go to bed.
But I don't have my teddy.

So I have my teddy.
But I don't have my bunny.

So I have my teddy and my bunny.
But I don't have my duck.

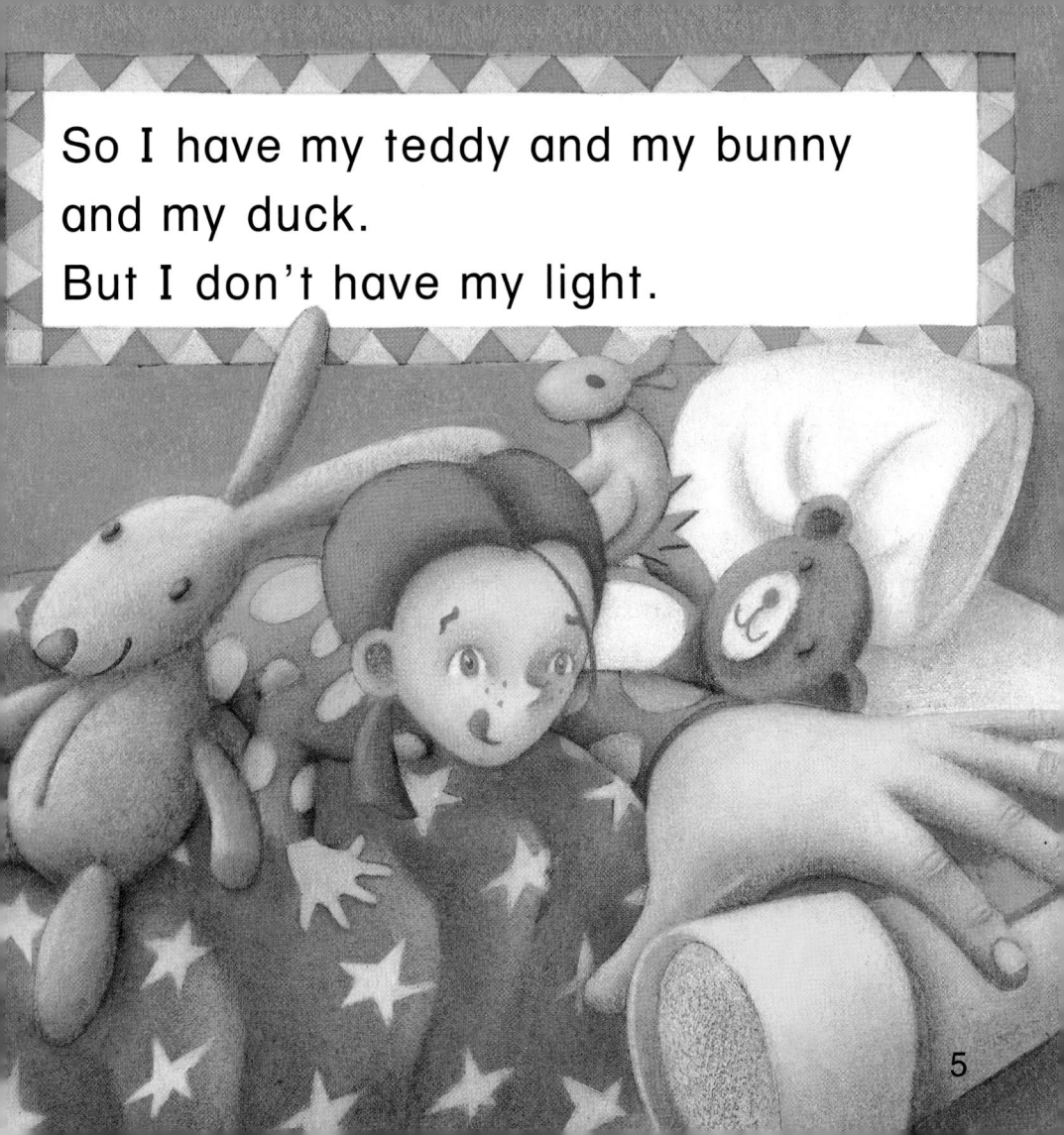

So I have my teddy and my bunny
and my duck.
But I don't have my light.

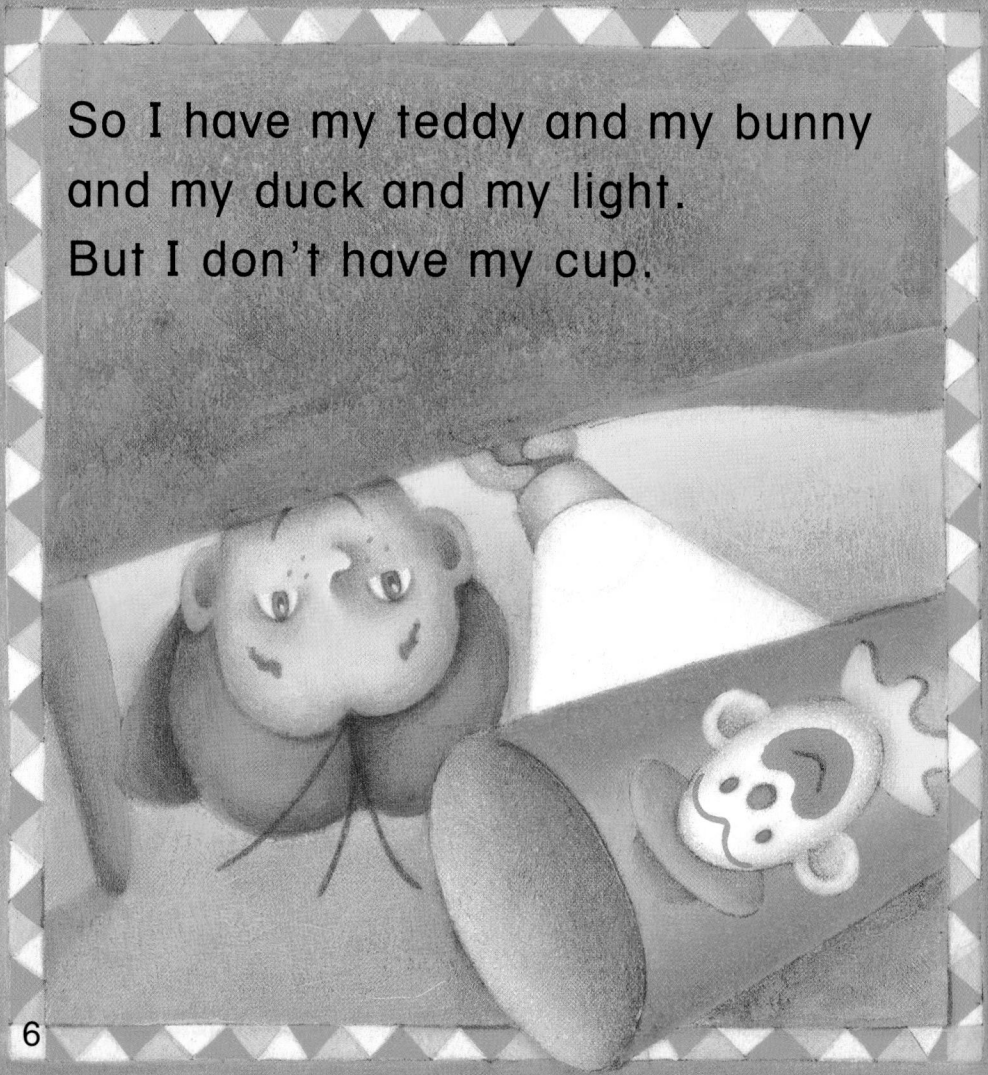

So I have my teddy and my bunny
and my duck and my light.
But I don't have my cup.

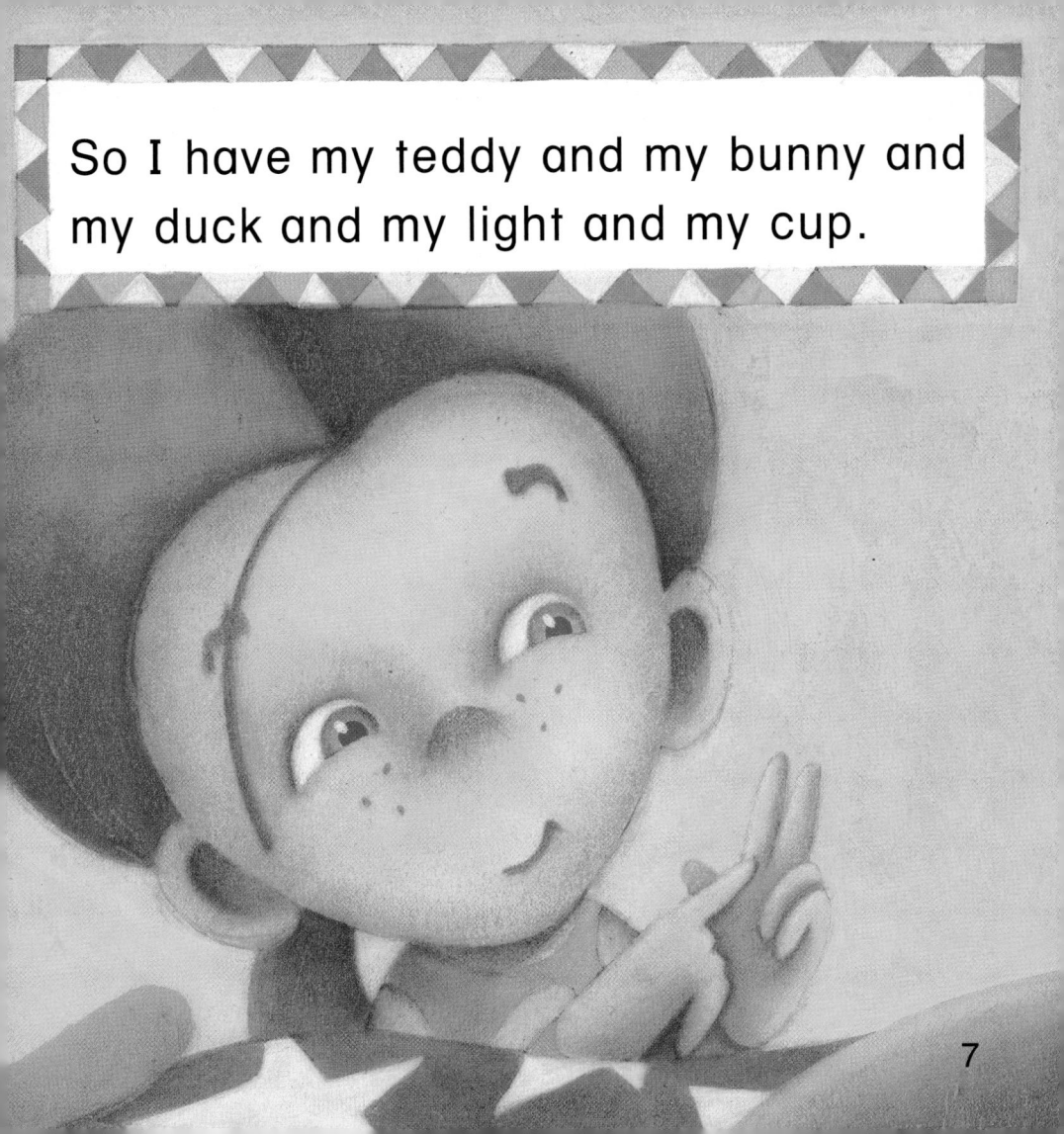

So I have my teddy and my bunny and my duck and my light and my cup.

I was just about to go to bed.
But I don't have a bed!